"Trickle Down" Theory and "Tax Cuts for the Rich"

Thomas Sowell

HOOVER INSTITUTION PRESS

STANFORD UNIVERSITY   STANFORD, CALIFORNIA

The Hoover Institution on War, Revolution and Peace, founded at Stanford University in 1919 by Herbert Hoover, who went on to become the thirty-first president of the United States, is an interdisciplinary research center for advanced study on domestic and international affairs. The views expressed in its publications are entirely those of the authors and do not necessarily reflect the views of the staff, officers, or Board of Overseers of the Hoover Institution.

www.hoover.org

Hoover Institution Press Publication No. 635

Hoover Institution at Leland Stanford Junior University,
Stanford, California 94305-6010

First printing 2012
18 17 16 15 14   8 7 6 5 4 3

Manufactured in the United States of America

The paper used in this publication meets the minimum Requirements of the American National Standard for Information Sciences—Permanence of Paper for Printed Library Materials, ANSI/NISO Z39.48-1992. ♾

Cataloging-in-Publication Data is available from the Library of Congress.
ISBN: 978-0-8179-1615-2 (pbk. : alk. paper)
ISBN: 978-0-8179-1616-9 (e-book)

We fight for and against not men and things as they are, but for and against the caricatures we make of them.

J.A. Schumpeter[1]

At various times and places, particular individuals have argued that existing tax *rates* are so high that the government could collect more tax *revenues* if it lowered those tax rates, because the changed incentives would lead to more economic activity, resulting in more tax revenues out of rising incomes, even though the tax rate was lowered. This is clearly a testable hypothesis that people might argue for or against, on either empirical or analytical grounds. But that is seldom what happens.

Even when the particular tax cut proposal is to cut tax rates in all income brackets, including reducing tax rates by a higher percentage in the lower income brackets than in the upper income brackets, such proposals have nevertheless often been characterized by their opponents as "tax cuts for the rich" because the total amount of money saved by someone in the upper income brackets is often larger than the total amount of money saved by someone in the lower brackets. Moreover, the reasons for proposing such tax cuts are often verbally transformed from those of the advocates— namely, changing economic behavior in ways that generate more output, income and resulting higher tax revenues— to a very different theory attributed to the advocates by the opponents, namely "the trickle-down theory."

No such theory has been found in even the most voluminous and learned histories of economic theories, including J.A. Schumpeter's monumental 1,260-page *History of Economic Analysis*. Yet this non-existent theory* has become the object of denunciations from the pages of the *New York Times* and the *Washington Post* to the political arena. It has been attacked by Professor Paul Krugman of Princeton and Professor Peter Corning of Stanford, among others, and similar attacks have been repeated as far away as India.[2] It is a classic example of arguing against a caricature instead of confronting the argument actually made.

While arguments for cuts in high tax rates have often been made by free-market economists or by conservatives in the American sense, such arguments have also sometimes been made by people who were neither, including John Maynard Keynes[3] and Democratic Presidents Woodrow Wilson[4] and John F. Kennedy.[5] But the claim that these are "tax cuts for the rich," based on a "trickle-down theory" also has a long pedigree.

President Franklin D. Roosevelt's speech writer Samuel Rosenman referred to "the philosophy that had prevailed in Washington since 1921, that the object of government was to provide prosperity for those who lived and worked at the top of the economic pyramid, in the belief that prosperity would trickle down to the bottom of the heap and benefit all."[6] The same theme was repeated in the election campaign of 2008, when presidential candidate Barack Obama attacked what he called "the economic philosophy" which "says we should give more and more to those with the most and hope that prosperity trickles down to everyone else."[7]

When Samuel Rosenman referred to what had been happening "since 1921," he was referring to the series of tax rate reductions advocated by Secretary of the Treasury Andrew Mellon, and enacted into law by Congress during the decade of the 1920s. But the actual arguments advocated by Secretary Mellon had nothing to do with a "trickle-down theory." Mellon pointed out that, under the high income tax rates at the end of the Woodrow Wilson administration in 1921, vast sums of money had been put into tax shelters such as tax-exempt municipal bonds, instead of being invested in the private economy, where this money would create

---

* Some years ago, in my syndicated column, I challenged anyone to name any economist, of any school of thought, who had actually advocated a "trickle down" theory. No one quoted any economist, politician or person in any other walk of life who had ever advocated such a theory, even though many readers named someone who claimed that someone else had advocated it, without being able to quote anything actually said by that someone else.

more output, incomes and jobs.[8] It was an argument that would be made at various times over the years by others— and repeatedly evaded by attacks on a "trickle-down" theory found only in the rhetoric of opponents.

What actually followed the cuts in tax rates in the 1920s were rising output, rising employment to produce that output, rising incomes as a result and rising tax *revenues* for the government because of the rising incomes, even though the tax *rates* had been lowered. Another consequence was that people in higher income brackets not only paid a larger total amount of taxes, but a higher percentage of all taxes, after what have been called "tax cuts for the rich." There were somewhat similar results in later years after high tax rates were cut during the John F. Kennedy, Ronald Reagan and George W. Bush administrations.[9] After the 1920s tax cuts, it was not simply that investors' incomes rose but that this was now *taxable* income, since the lower tax rates made it profitable for investors to get higher returns by investing outside of tax shelters.

The facts are unmistakably plain, for those who bother to check the facts. In 1921, when the tax rate on people making over $100,000 a year was 73 percent, the federal government collected a little over $700 million in income taxes, of which 30 percent was paid by those making over $100,000. By 1929, after a series of tax rate reductions had cut the tax rate to 24 percent on those making over $100,000, the federal government collected more than a billion dollars in income taxes, of which 65 percent was collected from those making over $100,000.[10]

There is nothing mysterious about this. Under the sharply rising tax rates during the Woodrow Wilson administration, to pay for the First World War, fewer and fewer people reported high taxable incomes, whether by putting their money into tax-exempt securities or by any of the other ways of rearranging their financial affairs to minimize their tax liability. Under these escalating wartime income tax rates, the number of people reporting taxable incomes of more than $300,000— a huge sum in the money of that era— declined from well over a thousand in 1916 to fewer than three hundred in 1921. The total amount of taxable income earned by people making over $300,000 declined by more than four-fifths during those years.[11] Since these were years of generally rising incomes, as Mellon pointed out, there was no reason to believe that the wealthy were suddenly suffering drastic reductions in their own incomes,[12] but considerable reason to believe that they were receiving tax-exempt incomes that did not have to be reported under existing laws at that time.

By the Treasury Department's estimate, the money invested in tax-exempt securities had nearly tripled in a decade.[13] The total estimated value of these securities was almost three times the size of the federal government's annual budget, and more than half as large as the national debt.[14] In short, these were sums of money with great potential impact on the economy, depending on where they were invested.

Andrew Mellon pointed out that "the man of large income has tended more and more to invest his capital in such a way that the tax collector cannot reach it."[15] The value of tax-exempt securities, he said, "will be greatest in the case of the wealthiest taxpayer" and will be "relatively worthless" to a small investor, so that the cost of making up such tax losses by the government must fall on those other, non-wealthy taxpayers "who do not or cannot take refuge in tax-exempt securities."[16] Mellon called it an "almost grotesque" result to have "higher taxes on all the rest in order to make up the resulting deficiency in the revenues."[17]

Secretary Mellon repeatedly sought to get Congress to end tax-exemptions for municipal bonds and other securities,[18] pointing out the inefficiencies in the economy that such securities created.[19] He also found it "repugnant" in a democracy that there should be "a class in the community which cannot be reached for tax purposes."[20] Secretary Mellon said: "It is incredible that a system of taxation which permits a man with an income of $1,000,000 a year to pay not one cent to the support of his Government should remain unaltered."[21]

Congress, however, refused to put an end to tax-exempt securities.* They continued what Mellon called the "gesture of taxing the rich," while in fact high tax rates on paper were "producing less and less

---

* However economically inconsistent it was to have very high tax rates on high incomes, while providing a large loophole through which the wealthy could avoid paying those taxes, it was politically beneficial to elected officials, who could attract votes with class-warfare rhetoric and at the same time attract donations from the wealthy by providing an easy escape from actually paying those taxes— and sometimes any taxes at all.

revenue each year and at the same time discouraging industry and threatening the country's future prosperity."[22] Unable to get Congress to end what he called "the evil of tax-exempt securities,"[23] Secretary Mellon sought to reduce the incentives for investors to divert their money from productive investments in the economy to putting it into safe havens in these tax shelters:

> Just as labor cannot be forced to work against its will, so it can be taken for granted that capital will not work unless the return is worth while. It will continue to retire into the shelter of tax-exempt bonds, which offer both security and immunity from the tax collector.[24]

In other words, high tax rates *that many people avoid paying* do not necessarily bring in as much revenue to the government as lower tax rates that more people are in fact paying, when these lower tax rates make it safe to invest their money where they can get a higher rate of return in the economy than they get from tax-exempt securities. The facts are plain: There were 206 people who reported annual taxable incomes of one million dollars or more in 1916. But, as the tax rates rose, that number fell drastically, to just 21 people by 1921. Then, after a series of tax rate cuts during the 1920s, the number of individuals reporting taxable incomes of a million dollars or more rose again to 207 by 1925.[25] Under these conditions, it should not be surprising that the government collected more tax revenue after tax rates were cut. Nor is it surprising that, with increased economic activity following the shift of vast sums of money from tax shelters into the productive economy, the annual unemployment rate from 1925 through 1928 ranged from a high of 4.2 percent to a low of 1.8 percent.[26]

The point here is not simply that the weight of evidence is on one side of the argument rather than the other but, more fundamentally, that *there was no serious engagement with the arguments actually advanced* but instead an evasion of those arguments by depicting them as simply a way of transferring tax burdens from the rich to other taxpayers. What Senators Robert La Follette and Burton K. Wheeler said in their political campaign literature during the 1924 election campaign— that "the Mellon tax plan" was "a device to relieve multimillionaires at the expense of other tax payers," and "a master effort of the special privilege mind," to "tax the poor and relieve the rich"[27]— would become perennial features of both intellectual and political discourse to the present day.

Even in the twenty-first century, the same arguments used by opponents of tax cuts in the 1920s were repeated in the book *Winner-Take-All Politics*, whose authors refer to "the 'trickle-down' scenario that advocates of helping the have-it-alls with tax cuts and other goodies constantly trot out."[28] No one who actually trotted out any such scenario was cited, much less quoted.

Repeatedly, over the years, the arguments of the proponents and opponents of tax rate reductions have been arguments about two fundamentally different things. Proponents of tax rate cuts base their arguments on anticipated *changes in behavior* by investors in response to reduced income tax rates. Opponents of tax cuts attribute to the proponents a desire to see higher income taxpayers have more after-tax income, so that their prosperity will somehow "trickle down" to others, which opponents of tax cuts deny will happen. One side is talking about behavioral changes that can change the total output of the economy, while the other side is talking about changing the direction of existing after-tax income flows among people of differing income levels at existing levels of output. These have been arguments about very different things, and the two arguments have largely gone past each other untouched.

Although Secretary of the Treasury Andrew Mellon was the key figure in getting tax rates lowered in the 1920s, he was by no means the only, or the first, person to make the argument that tax rates can be so high as to fail to bring in more revenue. Members of both Democratic and Republican administrations made that argument, as Mellon pointed out.[29]

During the preceding Democratic administration of Woodrow Wilson, Secretary of the Treasury Carter Glass said of tax rates in 1919 that "the only consequence of any further increase would be to drive possessors of these great incomes more and more to place their wealth in the billions of dollars of wholly exempt securities."[30] Driving the money of wealthy investors into tax-exempt state and municipal bonds had consequences for both the federal government's tax revenue and for the economy in general, as Secretary Glass spelled out:

> This process not only destroys a source of revenue to the Federal Government, but tends to withdraw the capital of very rich men from the development of new enterprises and place it at the disposal of State and municipal governments upon terms so easy to them . . . as to stimulate wasteful and nonproductive expenditure by State and municipal governments.[31]

One year later, another Secretary of the Treasury in the Woodrow Wilson administration made essentially the same argument, saying that high taxes on high incomes "have passed the point of maximum productivity and are rapidly driving the wealthier taxpayers to transfer their investments into the thousands of millions of tax-free securities which compete so disastrously with the industrial and railroad securities upon the ready purchase of which the development of industry and the expansion of foreign trade intimately depend."[32] Secretary David Franklin Houston pointed out that the taxable income of people who earned $300,000 and up in 1916 had been more than cut in half by 1918— not because he thought their total incomes had gone down but "almost certainly through investment by the richer taxpayers in tax-exempt properties."[33]

President Woodrow Wilson made a very similar argument in his 1919 message to Congress:

> The Congress might well consider whether the higher rates of income and profits taxes can in peace times be effectively productive of revenue, and whether they may not, on the contrary, be destructive of business activity and productive of waste and inefficiency. There is a point at which in peace times high rates of income and profits taxes discourage energy, remove the incentive to new enterprise, encourage extravagant expenditures, and produce industrial stagnation with consequent unemployment and other attendant evils.[34]

At this point, there was not yet a sharp and pervasive partisan difference on either the desirability of lowering high tax rates on high-income taxpayers or on the reasons for doing so. Nor did either party argue that lower tax rates would create prosperity at the top that would "trickle down" to others. President Calvin Coolidge was in fact quite explicit that the primary purpose of lowering tax rates was for the government to collect more tax revenues:

> The first object of taxation is to secure revenue. When the taxation of large incomes is approached with this in view, the problem is to find a rate which will produce the largest returns. Experience does not show that the higher rate produces the larger revenue. . . .
>
> I agree perfectly with those who wish to relieve the small taxpayer by getting the largest possible contribution from the people with large incomes. But if the rates on large incomes are so high that they disappear, the small taxpayer will be left to bear the entire burden.[35]

Although there were some political attacks in the 1920s on Mellon's tax-cutting plans, there was not yet the utter political polarization over "tax cuts for the rich" that characterized the later years of the twentieth century and the early years of the twenty-first. Nor was there the same ideological polarization in earlier times. It was none other than John Maynard Keynes who said, in 1933, that "taxation may be so high as to defeat its object," that "given sufficient time to gather the fruits, a reduction of taxation will run a better chance, than an increase, of balancing the Budget."[36]

In 1962, Democratic President John F. Kennedy, like both Democratic and Republican Presidents and Secretaries of the Treasury in earlier years, pointed out that "it is a paradoxical truth that tax rates are too high today and tax revenues are too low and the soundest way to raise the revenues in the long run is to cut the rates now." This was because investors' "efforts to avoid tax liabilities" make "certain types of less productive activity more profitable than other more valuable undertakings" and "this inhibits our growth and efficiency." Therefore the "purpose of cutting taxes" is "to achieve the more prosperous, expanding economy."[37] ***Total output and economic growth*** were italicized words in the text of John F. Kennedy's address to Congress in January 1963, urging cuts in tax rates.[38] In short, President Kennedy was talking about inducing changes in behavior designed to increase aggregate output, not changing the allocation of existing income flows, in hopes that more prosperity at the top would "trickle down."

Much the same theme was repeated yet again in President Ronald Reagan's February 1981 address to a joint session of Congress, pointing out that "this is not merely a shift of wealth between different sets of taxpayers." Instead, basing himself on a "solid body of economic experts," he expected that "real production in goods and services will grow."[39] In short, President Reagan was likewise not talking about after-tax income flows but about changes in behavior anticipated to increase aggregate output in the wake of changing tax rates. In 2001, President George W. Bush proposed his tax rate cuts, citing the Kennedy administration and Reagan administration precedents.[40]

In short, neither these earlier nor later arguments for cuts in tax rates had anything to do with making some people more prosperous, so that their prosperity might "trickle down" to others. But empirical evidence on what was actually said and done, as well as the actual consequences of tax cuts in four different administrations over a span of more than eighty years have also been largely ignored by those opposed to what they call "tax cuts for the rich."

Confusion between reducing tax *rates* on individuals and reducing tax *revenues* received by the government has run through much of these discussions over these many years. Famed historian Arthur M. Schlesinger, Jr., for example, said that although Andrew Mellon advocated balancing the budget and paying off the national debt, he "inconsistently" sought a "reduction of tax rates."[41] In reality, the national debt was reduced, as more revenue came into the government under the lowered tax rates. The national debt was just under $24 billion in 1921 and it was reduced to under $18 billion in 1928.[42] Nor was

Professor Schlesinger the only highly regarded historian to perpetuate economic confusion between tax rates and tax revenues.

Today, widely used textbooks, written by various well-known historians, have continued to grossly misstate what was advocated in the 1920s and what the actual consequences were. According to the textbook **These United States** by Pulitzer Prize winner Professor Irwin Unger of New York University, Secretary of the Treasury Andrew Mellon, "a rich Pittsburgh industrialist," persuaded Congress to "reduce income tax rates at the upper levels while leaving those at the bottom untouched." Thus "Mellon won further victories for his drive to shift more of the tax burden from high-income earners to the middle and wage-earning classes."[43] But hard data show that, in fact, both the amount and the proportion of taxes paid by those whose net income was no higher than $25,000 went *down* between 1921 and 1929, while both the amount and the proportion of taxes paid by those whose net incomes were between $50,000 and $100,000 went up— and the amount and proportion of taxes paid by those whose net incomes were over $100,000 went up even more sharply.[44]

Another widely used textbook, co-authored by a number of distinguished historians, two of whom won Pulitzer Prizes, said of Andrew Mellon: "It was better, he argued, to place the burden of taxes on lower-income groups" and that a "share of the tax-free profits of the rich, Mellon reassured the country, would ultimately trickle down to the middle- and lower-income groups in the form of salaries and wages."[45] What Mellon actually said was that tax policy "must lessen, so far as possible, the burden of taxation on those least able to bear it."[46] He therefore proposed sharper percentage cuts in tax rates at the lower income levels[47]— and that was done. Mellon also proposed eliminating federal taxes on movie tickets, on grounds that such taxes were paid by "the great bulk of the people whose main source of recreation is attending the movies in the neighborhood of their homes."[48] In short, Mellon advocated the direct opposite of the policies attributed to him.

The very idea that profits "trickle down" to workers depicts the economic sequence of events in the opposite order from that in the real world. Workers must first be hired, and commitments made to pay them, *before* there is any output produced to sell for a profit, and independently of whether that output subsequently sells for a profit or at a loss. With many investments, whether they lead to a profit or a loss can often be determined only years later, and workers have to be paid in the meantime, rather than waiting for profits to "trickle down" to them. The real effect of tax rate reductions is to make the *future prospects* of profit look more favorable, leading to more *current* investments that generate more current economic activity and more jobs.

Those who attribute a trickle-down theory to others are attributing their own misconception to others, as well as distorting both the arguments used and the hard facts about what actually happened after the recommended policies were put into effect.

Another widely used history textbook, a best-seller titled *The American Nation* by Professor John Garraty of Columbia University, said that Secretary Mellon "opposed lower rates for taxpayers earning less than $66,000."[49] Still another best-selling textbook, *The American Pageant* with multiple authors, declared: "Mellon's spare-the-rich policies thus shifted much of the tax burden from the wealthy to the middle-income groups."[50]

There is no need to presume that the scholars who wrote these history textbooks were deliberately lying, in order to protect a vision or an agenda. They may simply have relied on a peer consensus so widely held and so often repeated as to be seen as "well-known facts" requiring no serious re-examination. The results show how unreliable peer consensus can be, even when it is a peer consensus of highly intellectual people, if those people share a very similar vision of the world and treat its conclusions as axioms, rather than as hypotheses that need to be checked against facts. These history textbooks may also reflect the economic illiteracy of many leading scholars outside the field of economics, who nevertheless insist on proclaiming their conclusions on economic issues.

When widely recognized scholars have been so cavalier, it is hardly surprising that the media have followed suit. For example, *New York Times* columnist Tom Wicker called the Reagan administration's tax cuts "the old Republican 'trickle-down' faith."[51] *Washington Post* columnist David S. Broder called these tax cuts "feeding the greed of the rich" while "adding to the pain of the poor"— part of what he called the "moral meanness of the Reagan administration."[52] Under the headline, "Resurrection of Coolidge," another *Washington Post* columnist, Haynes Johnson, characterized the Reagan tax rate cuts as part of the "help-the-rich-first, and let-the-rest-trickle-down philosophies."[53]

John Kenneth Galbraith characterized the "trickle-down effect" as parallel to "the horse-and-sparrow metaphor, holding that if the horse is fed enough oats, some will pass through to the road for the sparrows."[54] Similar characterizations of a "trickle-down" theory were common in op-ed columns by Leonard Silk, Alan Brinkley and other well-known writers of the time, as well as in *New York Times* editorials.[55]

Responses to later tax cut proposals during the George W. Bush administration included denunciations of "trickle-down" economics from, among others, Arthur M. Schlesinger, Jr., Paul Krugman, and Jonathan Chait. *Washington Post* columnist David S. Broder denounced "the financial bonanza that awaits the wealthiest Americans in the Bush plan."[56]

Implicit in the approach of both academic and media critics of what they call "tax cuts for the rich" and a "trickle-down theory" is a zero-sum conception of the economy, where the benefits of some come at the expense of others. That those with such a zero-sum conception of the economy often show little or no interest in the factors affecting the creation of wealth— as distinguished from their preoccupation with its distribution— is consistent with their vision, however inconsistent it is with the views of others who are focussed on the growth of the economy, as emphasized by both Presidents John F. Kennedy and Ronald Reagan, for example.

What is also inconsistent is attributing one's own assumptions to those who are arguing on the basis of entirely different assumptions. Challenging those other assumptions, or the conclusions which derive from them, on either analytical or empirical grounds would be legitimate, but simply attributing to them arguments that they never made is not.

Even when empirical evidence substantiates the arguments made for cuts in tax rates, such facts are not treated as evidence relevant to testing a disputed hypothesis, but as isolated curiosities. Thus, when tax revenues rose in the wake of the tax rate cuts made during the George W. Bush administration, the *New York Times* reported: "An unexpectedly steep rise in tax revenues from corporations and the wealthy is driving down the projected budget deficit this year."[57] Expectations, of course, are in the eye of the beholder. However surprising the increases in tax revenues may have been to the *New York Times*, they are exactly what proponents of reducing high tax rates have been expecting, not only from these particular tax rate cuts, but from similar reductions in high tax rates at various times going back more than three-quarters of a century.

To the extent that the American economy has changed since the time of Andrew Mellon, it has changed in ways that make it even easier for wealthy investors to escape high tax rates. A globalized economy makes overseas investments a readily available alternative to buying tax-exempt bonds domestically. Even if the domestic tax rate is not "high" by historic standards, what matters now is whether it is high compared to tax rates in other countries to which large sums of money can be readily sent electronically. Meanwhile, unemployed workers cannot nearly so readily relocate to other countries to take the jobs created there by American investments fleeing higher tax rates at home.

NOTES

1. J.A. Schumpeter, *History of Economic Analysis* (New York: Oxford University Press, 1954), p. 90.

2. See, for example, "Fuzzy Economic Thinking; Job Czar for the Jobless," *New York Times*, September 3, 2003, p. A18; "Yo-Yo Economics," *Washington Post*, May 23, 2003, p. A24; Robert H. Frank, "In the Real World of Work and Wages, Trickle-Down Theories Don't Hold Up," *New York Times*, April 12, 2007, p. C3; Paul Krugman, "The Hostage Economy," *New York Times*, March 28, 2001, p. A21; Peter Corning, *The Fair Society: The Science of Human Nature and the Pursuit of Social Justice* (Chicago: University of Chicago Press, 2011), p. 117; Amity Shlaes, *The Forgotten Man: A New History of the Great Depression* (New York: HarperCollins, 2007), p. 128; S.M. Michael, editor, *Dalits in Modern India* (New Delhi:Vistaar Publications, 1999), p. 288.

3. John Maynard Keynes, "The Means to Prosperity," *The Means to Prosperity*, by J.M. Keynes, et al., (Buffalo: Economica Books, 1959), p. 11.

4. Woodrow Wilson, *The Hope of the World* (New York: Harper & Brothers, 1920), pp. 185–186.

5. *Public Papers of the Presidents of the United States: John F. Kennedy, 1962* (Washington: U.S. Government Printing Office, 1963), p. 879.

6. Amity Shlaes, *The Forgotten Man*, p. 128. Much the same argument was made even earlier, in William Jennings Bryan's famous "cross of gold" speech in 1896.

7. M. Jay Wells, "Why the Mortgage Crisis Happened," *Investor's Business Daily*, October 30, 2008, p. A1.

8. Andrew W. Mellon, *Taxation: The People's Business* (New York: The Macmillan Company, 1924), pp. 127–138, 199–204.

9. James Gwartney and Richard Stroup, "Tax Cuts: Who Shoulders the Burden?" *Federal Reserve Bank of Atlanta Economic Review*, March 1982, pp. 19–27;

Benjamin G. Rader, "Federal Taxation in the 1920s: A Re-examination," *Historian*, Vol. 33, No. 3, p. 433; Robert L. Bartley, *The Seven Fat Years: And How to Do It Again* (New York: The Free Press, 1992), pp. 71–74; Burton W. Folsom, Jr., *The Myth of the Robber Barons: A New Look at the Rise of Big Business in America*, sixth edition (Herndon, VA: Young America's Foundation, 2010), pp. 108, 116; Adrian Dungan and Kyle Mudry, "Individual Income Tax Rates and Shares, 2007," *Statistics of Income Bulletin*, Winter 2010, p. 63.

10. Benjamin G. Rader, "Federal Taxation in the 1920s: A Re-examination," *Historian*, Vol. 33, No. 3, pp. 432–433.

11. Andrew W. Mellon, *Taxation*, pp. 72, 74.

12. Ibid., p. 76.

13. Ibid., p. 201.

14. Burton W. Folsom, Jr., *The Myth of the Robber Barons*, sixth edition, p. 109.

15. Andrew W. Mellon, *Taxation*, p. 72.

16. Ibid., pp. 152, 158.

17. Ibid., p. 160.

18. Ibid., pp. 79–80, 141–142, 171–172.

19. Ibid., pp. 13, 15–16, 81–82, 141–142.

20. Ibid., p. 170.

21. Ibid., p. 79.

22. Ibid., pp. 106–107.

23. Ibid., p. 167.

24. Ibid., p. 79.

25. Treasury Department, U.S. Internal Revenue, *Statistics of Income from Returns of Net Income for 1925* (Washington: U.S. Government Printing Office, 1927), p. 21.

26. U.S. Bureau of the Census, *Historical Statistics of the United States: Colonial Times to 1970* (Washington: Government Printing Office, 1975), Part 1, p. 126.

27. *The Facts: La Follette-Wheeler Campaign Text-Book* (Chicago: LaFollette-Wheeler Campaign Headquarters, 1924), pp. 77, 80, 81.

28. Jacob S. Hacker and Paul Pierson, *Winner-Take-All Politics: How Washington Made the Rich Richer— and Turned Its Back on the Middle Class* (New York: Simon and Schuster, 2010), p. 20.

29. Andrew W. Mellon, *Taxation*, pp. 10–11, 127, 180, 219–220.

30. *Annual Report of the Secretary of the Treasury on the State of the Finances for the Fiscal Year Ended June 30, 1919* (Washington: Government Printing Office, 1920), p. 24.

31. Ibid.

32. *Annual Report of the Secretary of the Treasury on the State of the Finances for the Fiscal Year Ended June 30, 1920* (Washington: Government Printing Office, 1921), p. 36.

33. Ibid., pp. 36–37.

34. Woodrow Wilson, *The Hope of the World*, pp. 185–186.

35. "Text of President's Speech Elaborating His Views," *Washington Post*, February 13, 1924, p. 4.

36. John Maynard Keynes, "The Means to Prosperity," *The Means to Prosperity*, by J.M. Keynes, et al., p. 11.

37. *Public Papers of the Presidents of the United States: John F. Kennedy, 1962*, pp. 878–880, *passim*. In a similar vein, decades earlier Andrew Mellon deplored the "flight of capital into safe but unproductive forms of investment." Andrew W. Mellon, *Taxation*, p. 93.

38. "Special Message to the Congress on Tax Reduction and Reform," January 24, 1963, *Public Papers of the Presidents of the United States: John F. Kennedy, 1963* (Washington: U.S. Government Printing Office, 1964), p. 75.

39. "Address Before a Joint Session of the Congress on the Program for Economic Recovery," *Public Papers of the Presidents of the United States: Ronald Reagan, 1981* (Washington: U.S. Government Printing Office, 1982), pp. 112, 113.

40. *Public Papers of the Presidents of the United States: George W. Bush, 2001* (Washington: U.S. Government Printing Office, 2003), pp. 144–145.

41. Arthur M. Schlesinger, Jr., *The Age of Roosevelt: The Crisis of the Old Order, 1919–1933* (Boston: Houghton Mifflin Company, 1957), p. 62.

42. U.S. Bureau of the Census, *Historical Statistics of the United States: Colonial Times to 1970*, Part 2, p. 1117.

43. Irwin Unger, *These United States: The Questions of Our Past*, concise edition (Upper Saddle River, NJ: Prentice-Hall, 1999), p. 591.

44. Burton W. Folsom, Jr., *The Myth of the Robber Barons*, sixth edition, p. 116.

45. John M. Blum, et al., *The National Experience: A History of the United States*, eighth edition (New York: Harcourt, Brace and Jovanovich, 1991), p. 640.

46. Andrew W. Mellon, *Taxation*, p. 9.

47. Ibid., pp. 54–57.

48. Ibid., pp. 61–62.

49. John A. Garraty, *The American Nation: A History of the United States* (New York: Harper & Row, 1966), p. 713.

50. Thomas A. Bailey, David M. Kennedy and Lizabeth Cohen, *The American Pageant: A History of the Republic*, eleventh edition (Boston: Houghton-Mifflin, 1998), p. 768.

51. Tom Wicker, "A Trojan Horse Indeed," *New York Times*, November 13, 1981, p. A35.

52. David S. Broder, "The Reagan Year: Conviction and Callousness," *Washington Post*, January 20, 1982, p. A23.

53. Haynes Johnson, "Resurrection of Coolidge— the Stamping of Nostalgia's Clay Feet," *Washington Post*, June 7, 1981, p. A3.

54. John Kenneth Galbraith, "The Heartless Society," *New York Times Magazine*, September 2, 1984, p. 44.

55. Leonard Silk, "A Tax Policy for the Rich," *New York Times*, June 12, 1981, p. D2; Alan Brinkley, "Calvin Reagan," *New York Times*, July 4, 1981, p. 19; Mark Green, "Economic Democracy," *New York Times*, March 7, 1982, p. E19; Ira C. Magaziner, "'Trickle Down' And Away," *New York Times*, May 25, 1982, p. A23; "After the Tax Spree," *New York Times*, July 29, 1981, p. A22; "There Is a Better Bet," *New York Times*, January 31, 1982, p. E20.

56. Arthur Schlesinger, Jr., "A Poor Tax Reduction Strategy," Letters to the Editor, *Washington Post*, March 25, 2001, p. B6; Paul Krugman, "The Hostage Economy," *New York Times*, March 28, 2001, p. A21; Jonathan Chait, "Going for Gold," *New Republic*, May 21, 2001, p. 25; David S. Broder, "Return to Reaganomics," *Washington Post*, February 6, 2001, p. A17.

57. Edmund L. Andrews, "Surprising Jump in Tax Revenues Curbs U.S. Deficit," *New York Times*, July 9, 2006, p. A1.